Are Early Warning Models
Still Useful Tools for Bank Supervisors?

Gary W. Whalen

Office of the Comptroller of the Currency

OCC Economics Working Paper 2010-3

December 2010

Keywords: Community banks; early warning; hazard model; risk.
JEL classifications: G21, G28, C41, C52.

Gary W. Whalen is a Senior Economic Advisor in the Policy Analysis Division of the Office of the Comptroller of the Currency, 250 E St. SW, Washington, DC 20219. Please address correspondence to the author (phone 202-874-4441; fax 202-874-5394; e-mail: gary.whalen@occ.treas.gov).

The views expressed in this paper are those of the author alone and do not necessarily reflect those of the Office of the Comptroller of the Currency or the U.S. Department of the Treasury. The author would like to thank Emily Gold and Janet Fix for their editorial assistance. The author takes responsibility for any errors.

Are Early Warning Models Still Useful Tools for Bank Supervisors?

Gary W. Whalen

December 2010

Abstract: This paper answers two timely, important research questions. Has the accuracy of statistical early warning models declined in recent years as the economic environment faced by banks has become more volatile? Has it become necessary to frequently respecify or re-estimate these models to produce reasonably accurate forecasts of bank risk?

To answer these questions, a set of Cox proportional hazard composite CAMELS[1] downgrade models are estimated for a sample of low-risk community banks at five different year-end dates ranging from 1997 through 2002. The estimated models are used to produce out-of-sample risk estimates for up to six future forecast periods. The models generally have Type I and Type II error rates in the low- to mid-30 percent range in each of the forecast years, including the most recent one. Forecast accuracy does not consistently or sharply decline with model age, indicating frequent respecification or re-estimation is unnecessary. In addition, a supplemental analysis of forecast accuracy indicates that a considerable number of banks categorized as Type II errors by the models in each forecast period appear to be high risk ex post. The implication is that the "true" Type II error rates of the models are lower than the conventional figures reported in the tables.

---

[1] CAMELS is an acronym for the risk assessment score assigned to banks by supervisors. The acronym reflects the component scores that are measures of a bank's capital adequacy, asset quality, management, earnings, liquidity, and sensitivity to market risk.

I. Introduction

Over the past 30 years, a great deal of research has investigated the potential usefulness of a variety of early warning models (EWM) as off-site supervisory tools. Accurate off-site models give bank supervisors the capability to identify high-risk banks in a timely manner before their financial conditions markedly deteriorate, in between expensive, time-consuming on-site examinations. This capability allows scarce examination resources to be used more efficiently and permits supervisory constraints to be imposed or rehabilitative strategies put in place expeditiously, reducing the risk of costly failures.

The performance of these models in the recent volatile financial environment is an important research topic. Specifically, does the accuracy of conventional EWMs estimated in more stable time periods decline markedly when economic conditions change significantly? Or is it necessary to respecify or re-estimate EWMs to obtain sufficiently accurate risk forecasts?

This paper examines the out-of-sample forecasting accuracy of a set of Cox proportional hazard composite CAMELS downgrade models for low-risk community national banks estimated at five different year-end dates ranging from 1997 through 2002.[2] The risk forecasts of these models are examined out-of-sample and compared with one another.

Briefly, when the predicted downgrade probabilities are used to identify the 500 riskiest banks in each forecast period, the conventional Type I and Type II error rates of all of the estimated models generally are in the low- to mid-30 percent range. This includes the most recent forecasting period, when 2007 data are used in the models to predict downgrades through the first quarter of 2010. Forecast accuracy does not consistently or sharply decline with model

---

[2] The CAMELS composite score is a numerical rating assigned by supervisors to reflect their assessment of the overall financial condition of a bank. The score takes on integer values ranging from 1 (best) to 5 (worst). For a more detailed discussion of the CAMELS score, see Feldman and Schmidt (1999).

age. This persistent level of accuracy suggests that relatively simple EWMs continue to be useful supervisory tools, even if they are not respecified or re-estimated frequently.

In addition, the supplemental analysis of forecast accuracy indicates that a considerable number of banks categorized as Type II errors by the models in each forecast period appear to be high risk ex post. The implication is that the "true" Type II error rates of the models are lower than the conventional figures reported in the tables.

In the next section, relevant studies are briefly reviewed. Section III details the construction of the Cox models used in the study. The estimation results are presented in section IV. Model forecasting accuracy is discussed in section V. Section VI presents a summary of the results and conclusions.

II. Short Review of Previous Research

Many previous studies have investigated EWMs for banks, but a hazard model approach was used in a relatively small number of them. Only four papers (Lane, Looney, and Wansley [1986]; Whalen [1991]; Gropp, Vesala, and Vulpes [2002]; and Whalen [2005]) are early warning studies, in which the focus is on developing and testing the out-of-sample accuracy of models designed to predict bank risk.[3] None of the studies thoroughly examines the relationship between model age and forecasting accuracy. The first two studies focus on bank failure and use models with a maximum time horizon of two years. In general, the set of independent variables found to be significant in these studies consists of ratios constructed from regulatory call reports that are standard indicators of various dimensions of bank risk.[4]

---

[3] In Fissel (1994), a bank failure model is estimated, but the focus of the paper is on using the model to develop fair risk-related deposit insurance premiums. In Wheelock and Wilson (2000), the focus is on explaining failure and acquisition in a competing risks framework.

[4] Whalen (1991) also found that the lagged percentage change in the state-level housing permits was a significant predictor of bank failure risk.

Unlike Lane, Looney and Wansley (1986) and Whalen (1991), Gropp et al. attempt to model the risk of a nonsupervisory ratings downgrade for a relatively small sample of European Union banks. More specifically, Gropp et al. define a downgrade as a reduction in a bank's Fitch-IBCA financial strength rating to a grade of C or below. Given the stated definition of a C-level rating, this dichotomy between low risk and high risk is very similar to the approach used in this paper.[5] The authors note the benefits of using such a risk measure in EWMs when failures are rare. They focus on whether variables constructed from equity and bond market price and yield data are useful leading indicators of the risk of publicly traded banks. They do not examine the classification accuracy of their estimated models out-of-sample.

Whalen (2005) develops a Cox proportional hazard model that is designed to predict the probability that a low-risk community bank will be downgraded to high-risk status over an eight-quarter time horizon. The risk dichotomy is made on the basis of CAMELS composite supervisory ratings, with a score of 2 separating the low and high-risk groups. The out-of-sample forecasting accuracy of the hazard model estimated at three different points in time is examined and compared with two simpler supervisory screens for only a single forecast period. In general, the hazard models are found to produce relatively accurate risk classifications out-of-sample. Model age does not appear to have a marked impact on classification accuracy. The hazard models are also found to be considerably more accurate than two simpler supervisory screens.

---

[5] A C-rated bank is defined as "an adequate bank that, however, possesses one or more troublesome aspects." See Gropp, Vesala, and Vulpes (2002), appendix 2: 53. Banks with composite ratings of 3 "exhibit some degree of supervisory concern in one or more … areas." See Federal Reserve System's *Commercial Bank Examination Manual* (1997): A.5020.1, 2. Available at http://www.federalreserve.gov/boarddocs/supmanual/cbem/cbem.pdf.

III. Construction of Cox CAMELS Downgrade Model

Measure of Risk

Statistical EWMs can be designed to produce estimates of a variety of indices of bank risk. Each of these potential risk measures has advantages and disadvantages. In this study, the target bank risk measure is based on supervisory ratings. More precisely, the model developed is designed to produce estimates of the probability that a low risk bank will be subsequently downgraded to high risk status over an eight-quarter time period. Banks are designated "low risk" if they have CAMELS composite scores of 1 or 2. Banks with composite CAMELS scores above 2 are classified as high risk.

There are advantages and disadvantages associated with using supervisory ratings-based measures of risk in a statistical EWM. The main advantage of this approach is that exam ratings are thought to be highly accurate measures of bank condition (at least of current condition) because they reflect supervisory assessments of private information (e.g., the quality of nontraded loans and an institution's management) that may be superior to that available to outside analysts. In addition, accurate CAMELS prediction or downgrade models are useful to supervisors. Identifying low-risk banks likely to be downgraded gives supervisors time to limit any moral hazard behavior or assist in the rehabilitation of institutions. Downgrade models might also be used to select the apparently low-risk banks that should be examined sooner rather than later. Another advantage of using supervisory ratings as the risk metric is that it permits model estimation in time periods in which other high-risk events like failure are rare.

There are also disadvantages to using supervisory assessments when modeling bank risk. Such ratings reflect subjective judgments on the part of examiners, and these judgments may differ across banks or change over time (e.g., banks in different size classes might be rated according to different criteria, or examination standards could change for all banks over time). In addition, the precise linkage between the ratings and expected conditions in the future can be unclear. For example, a composite score of 5 indicates a high likelihood of failure within a relatively short time, despite preventive measures. The signals provided by CAMELS scores of 3 and 4 are less clear, as is the incremental impact of moving up or down the rating scale by 1 or more rating points. Furthermore, when model predictions and actual ratings disagree, it is not clear which is the correct indicator of a bank's true risk.

Yet another potential problem, especially in the case of early warning hazard models that explicitly focus on the timing of the risk event, is that ratings reflect supervisory judgments about a bank's condition at a particular moment in time. Historically, such assessments have been made only on the basis of an on-site full-scope exam. Because such exams typically recur with a lag of four quarters or more, and the length of the lag might reflect any number of factors, the point when supervisors recognize a change in bank risk and revise a rating might not necessarily coincide closely with the moment when the change in risk could have been discerned if the bank were examined earlier. This problem, however, has been mitigated in recent years by the adoption of quarterly "periodic monitoring" of national banks by supervisors.[6] This monitoring can be off-site and can result in changes in supervisory ratings and on-site exam timing. As a result, exam ratings are likely to be better contemporaneous risk indicators than they have been in the past.

---

[6] For a description of the periodic monitoring process for national banks, see the "Community Bank Supervision" booklet of the OCC's *Comptroller's Handbook* (January 2010): 158–161. Available at www.occ.gov/static/publications/handbook/cbs.pdf.

Another potential problem with ratings-based risk measures is that it may be difficult to estimate reliable models during periods when there are few banks in some ratings classes or when few downgrades occur. This circumstance is not unique to this sort of risk measure, and in fact appears to be a much less serious problem, in recent periods, than if a failure-based risk measure were used instead.

In summary, a series of CAMELS downgrade models are estimated in this paper.[7] Each model generates estimates of the probability that a bank rated 1 or 2 at a given year-end will be subsequently downgraded to a rating of 3, 4, or 5 over the eight-quarter period beginning in the second quarter of the subsequent year.[8] In all of the time periods examined in this study, there were enough rating downgrades for reliable model estimates.

Hazard Downgrade Model

The focus of any hazard model is the time that elapses from the moment that observation of the sample subjects begins until some event of interest occurs, the subject exits the sample for some other reason, or the period of observation ends. Conventionally, subjects that experience the event of interest during the observation period are referred to as *failures*, and the time at which this occurs is referred to as time to failure. Conversely, those that do not fail over the entire observation period are referred to as *survivors*. Subjects that survive or disappear from the sample before the end of the observation period without experiencing the event of interest are referred to as *censored*.

The time to failure for the subjects in the sample is assumed to be a random variable with a probability distribution. The probability distribution of time to failure can be expressed in

---

different ways. One convenient way to express this distribution is through the related hazard function. A hazard function for a particular value of event time gives the instantaneous risk that an event will occur at the given time, t, for a subject with a given set of characteristics, given that the subject has not experienced the event prior to t.

A number of hazard models may be used in the analysis. They vary somewhat in form and make different assumptions about how the baseline hazard varies over time. This paper uses various estimated versions of a Cox proportional hazards model. In the case of a Cox model, the hazard function has the following general form:

(1) $\quad h(t|X_j) \;=\; h_0(t)\exp(X_j B)$

$h(t \mid X_j) =$ the instantaneous risk of an event for subject j at time t, given its relevant characteristics reflected in the set of variables included in X.

$h_0(t) =$ the baseline hazard for time period t

$X_j B =$ X_j represents a vector of variables describing relevant characteristics of subject j presumed to influence the hazard, and B represents a corresponding vector of weights that describe how each characteristic variable influences the hazard.

Another way to express this same probability distribution of event times is through the related survivor function. The survivor function gives the probability that a subject with a given set of relevant characteristics will not experience the event of interest through time t, or will "survive" beyond t. In the Cox model, the survivor function has the form given by equation 2:

(2)
$$S(t|X_j) = S_0(t)^{q_j}$$

$S(t | X_j) =$ the probability that subject j with characteristics given by X_j does not experience the event or survives through t, the chosen time horizon.

$S_0(t) =$ the "baseline" survival probability for the chosen time horizon t.

$q_j =$ an equation that incorporates the estimated coefficients or weights that describe how each included characteristic variable in X_j affects the probability that subject j survives beyond t.

The formula for q_j, in turn, is given in equation 3:

(3) $q_j = \exp(X_j B)$

where $X_j B$ has the same definition as it does in equation (1) above.

In the Cox model, the baseline hazard and survival probabilities are the same for all subjects and depend only on time. This specification implies that the ratio of the hazards of any two subjects is constant over time and is the reason this specification is called a proportional hazard model.[9] Model estimation generates the estimates of the baseline probabilities and the coefficients or weights on the characteristic variables that indicate the effect of each included variable on the likelihood that a subject experiences the event of interest. As a result, the expected signs of the variables in the survivor function appear to be counterintuitive. The estimation also provides measures of the statistical significance of each included characteristic variable and the entire set of variables taken together. This provides insight into the degree of confidence that can be placed on the coefficient estimates and the generated failure or survival probabilities that they imply.

---

[9] For a more complete discussion of hazard models, see Cleves, Gould, and Gutierrez (2002), Allison (1995), or Hosmer and Lemeshow (1999).

Using a hazard model rather than a binary logit model specification has several advantages. Unlike the logit model, hazard models take the timing of events over the interval of observation into account. Hazard models also permit the inclusion of subjects that are censored in the estimation sample. The Cox proportional hazard model also offers a potential advantage over alternative hazard models in that no assumption is made about how the baseline hazard varies over time.[10] This is appropriate in situations when there is no strong a priori reason to expect a particular relationship.[11]

In this paper the event of interest is the downgrade of a bank from low-risk (CAMELS 1 or 2) to high-risk status (CAMELS 3, 4, or 5) during the period of observation. Event time is measured in quarters. The estimated baseline survival probabilities and survivor functions are used to generate estimates of the likelihood that a sample bank with a given set of characteristics will not be downgraded to high-risk status through the end of each of eight quarters beginning one quarter after the end of the forecast year. Given any quarterly time horizon, lower estimated survival probabilities imply higher bank risk, while higher probabilities imply lower risk.

Data Sets Used to Estimate the Model

For simplicity and to permit a reasonable test of out-of-sample forecast accuracy, models are estimated using only year-end annual data for the explanatory variables. Separate models are estimated for 1997, 1999, 2000, 2001, and 2002. The estimation sample for each time period

---

[10] For example, the exponential model and Weibull model are also proportional hazard models but embody particular assumptions about the relationship between the hazard rate and time. In the former, the hazard is constant over time. In the latter, the relationship between the hazard and time can vary.

[11] Other types of hazard models, called parametric hazard models, exist where a specific relationship between the hazard and time are assumed. These sorts of models can produce more precise estimates of the effects of the included variables if the data are consistent with the assumed relationship.

consists of low-risk national banks with total assets of $1 billion or less.[12] Credit-card banks, banks in existence fewer than three years, and banks that were downgraded or disappeared during the first quarter of the subsequent year are excluded from the estimation samples.[13]

For each of the five year-end estimation dates, sample banks are followed over the eight-quarter period beginning with the second quarter of the subsequent year. Each bank in the sample was assigned an event time value representing the number of quarters that elapsed between the start of the interval and the quarter in which it was downgraded, disappeared, or ceased to be a national bank.[14] Banks that were not downgraded over the entire period were also treated as censored and assigned a maximum time value of eight quarters.[15]

Similar data sets are also constructed for each year-end from 2003 through 2007. These data sets are used to test the out-of-sample forecasting accuracy of the models estimated for the five earlier time periods.

Selection of Explanatory Variables Used in the Models

The primary aim of the paper is to investigate the out-of-sample forecasting accuracy of relatively simple, low-cost EWMs. Judgment, a modicum of preliminary statistical analysis, and examination of in-sample classification accuracy were used to cull a relatively small set of the most informative variables from a modest list of candidates used in previous empirical early warning studies in each estimation year. The final specification of the downgrade equation for

---

[12] The asset size cutoff is not adjusted for price changes over time.

[13] There are two reasons for excluding downgrades in the first quarter after the estimation date. One is the lag in the availability of the final call report data used to construct most of the explanatory variables. The other is the minimal practical value of predicting downgrades at this time horizon.

[14] Banks might disappear through merger, failure, or voluntary liquidation. A national bank also can switch to a state charter. When a bank change occurs, its CAMELS rating no longer is available. Both types of banks are treated as censored in the analysis.

[15] Technically, the latter two groups of banks are treated as censored in the analysis.

each time period consists of explanatory variables that were found to be individually and collectively significant, exhibited reasonable coefficient signs, and produced decent in-sample forecasts. A more detailed discussion of the signs and significance of the coefficients on the included variables are included in the following section.

IV. Hazard Model Estimates

Table 1 details the five estimated models. The first two columns, under the "1997 Model" heading, contain the results for the Cox downgrade model estimated using year-end 1997 data for the explanatory variables and downgrade information for the 1998:Q2–2000:Q1 interval. The "1999 Model" (year-end 1999 data and downgrade information for 2000:Q2–2002:Q1) results appear in the second two columns. These two models were estimated in Whalen (2005) and are used here unchanged. The remaining columns in table 1 show hazard models estimated using 2000, 2001, and 2002 values of the explanatory variables and corresponding downgrade data.

Table 1

Estimated Survivor Functions for Alternative Cox Proportional Hazard Models for CAMELS Downgrades

Variable	1997 Model		1999 Model		2000 Model		2001 Model		2002 Model	
	Coefficient	Z statistic	Coefficient	Z statistic	Coefficient	Z statistic	Coefficient	Z statistic	Coefficient	Z statistic
Capital adequacy										
Total equity/total assets	-0.183996	-4.73	-0.131210	-2.53			-0.1165469	-2.12	-0.165932	-3.06
Tangible equity/total assets										
Loan portfolio quality and composition										
Total noncurrent loans/total loans			0.406983	4.84	0.1799468	2.95	0.3035294	5.95	0.2351471	5.66
Loans 30-89 days past due/total loans			0.202640	3.34	0.3067569	6.41	0.2976348	4.97	0.2119726	2.92
Total nonperforming loans/total loans	0.214103	6.87								
Loan loss provision/total assets	0.398585	3.41	0.521865	4.91					0.3067955	2.41
Loan loss reserve/total loans			-0.446415	-2.20						
Total loans/total assets	0.047535	4.91	0.046174	4.63	0.019189	2.64			0.0167431	1.77
Commercial and industrial loans/total assets										
(Commercial and industrial loans and commercial real estate loans)/total assets										
Pretax net income/total assets	-0.194596	-4.13	-0.270941	-2.66	-0.390339	-4.62	-0.553446	-4.33	-0.301986	-4.16
Liability composition										
Nonmaturity deposits/total assets	-0.017326	-1.96	-0.016395	-1.98			-0.036596	-3.46	-0.027291	-2.37
Brokered deposits/total assets	0.113064	5.19	0.050417	1.80						
Other borrowed funds < 1 year/total assets	0.046632	2.50	-0.035877	-3.23	0.0979539	3.33	0.0837885	2.00	0.0667965	1.73
Total investment securities/total assets					-0.0422701	-4.17	-0.0418486	-4.10		
Interest rate risk										
Total loans with maturity/repricing >= 5 years/total assets					0.0222224	2.31	0.0228791	2.50		
Total assets with maturity/repricing >= 5 years/total assets										
Net gains on loan sales/total assets	0.829428	5.18								
Log total assets	-0.411710	-3.37	-0.379183	-2.95						
Dummy variable = 1 if management rating > CAMELS	0.829428	5.18	0.699482	1.78			0.9998734	2.76	0.7563433	1.73
Log likelihood	-719.37		-505.14		-631.74		-558.95		-475.82	
Likelihood ratio statistic*	176.4		146.41		138.46		132.1		89.41	
8-quarter baseline survival probability	0.9722		0.9794		0.9632		0.9747		0.9725	
Number of banks in estimation sample	2082		1823		1714		1653		1620	
Number of downgrades	107		78		95		85		71	

*This is a X^2 statistic with degrees of freedom equal to he number of explanatory variables included in the estimated equation.

12

The differences in the specifications for each time period are relatively modest, indicating that the downgrade models are somewhat but not completely stable. Still, a total of only 20 different explanatory variables appear in the five estimated equations. Some variability in specifications across the five models may simply reflect the effects of multicollinearity. A more informative test of the effects of model instability is the relative forecasting accuracy of the alternative model specifications out-of-sample, which is examined below.

Almost all of the explanatory variables appearing in the models are ratios constructed from regulatory call reports filed by all banks. Most of these ratios, or some related variant, consistently appear in many of the models estimated in previous empirical studies because they reflect alternative dimensions of bank risk that should be captured in CAMELS composite scores.

In table 1, the first two variables used in the models are alternative indicators of bank capital adequacy. The first is the ratio of total equity to total assets. The second simply substitutes tangible equity capital in the numerator. The risk of a downgrade should be lower for banks with higher capital ratios, so the coefficients on the two capital measures in the estimated equations should be negative.

The next eight explanatory variables in the table are indicators of credit risk. The first of these ratios is total noncurrent loans divided by total loans.[16] The second is loans past due 30–89 days divided by total loans. The third, total nonperforming loans relative to total loans, is simply the sum of the previous two ratios. Preliminary results supported the use of the disaggregated components in all of the years except 1997.

The next of the credit-risk variables is loan-loss provision divided by total assets. The fifth credit-risk variable is the reserve for loan losses divided by total loans. The sixth is the ratio

---

[16] Noncurrent loans are the sum of nonaccrual loans and loans past due 90 days or more.

of total loans to total assets. The seventh is total commercial and industrial (C&I) loans divided by total assets. The eighth and final credit-risk indicator includes both C&I and commercial real estate loans in the numerator.[17] Higher values of all of these variables except the loan-loss reserve measure imply greater credit risk. Because banks with more credit risk are more likely to be downgraded, the estimated coefficient on all of these variables except the loan-loss reserve ratio should be positive. A negative coefficient is expected on the loan-loss reserve ratio.

Table 1 lists one variable that is an indicator of profitability: pretax return on assets.[18] More profitable banks are less likely to be downgraded, so a negative coefficient on this variable is expected in the estimated equations.

The next four variables in table 1 are ratios that can be interpreted as measures of liquidity, although several might also be viewed as indicators of a bank's cost of funds. The first of these variables is total nonmaturity deposits divided by total assets.[19] The numerator of this ratio is the sum of transactions deposits, savings deposits, and money market deposit accounts (MMDA). Higher values of this ratio indicate greater bank liquidity and a lower downgrade risk, so the expected coefficient sign on this variable is negative. The next two variables are ratios that capture the extent to which a bank relies on more volatile liabilities for funding. One measure is brokered deposits divided by total assets; the other is borrowed funds with less than one year to maturity divided by total assets. Higher ratios of volatile liabilities imply less liquidity, a higher downgrade risk, and thus a positive estimated coefficient. The final liquidity indicator is total

---

[17] In all of the estimation years, the impacts of commercial real estate lending and the expected riskiest component of this activity, construction lending, were investigated but were never found to be significant separately.

[18] Pretax return on assets is used to avoid biases in the use of after-tax profitability measures given the increase in the number of the Subchapter S form by smaller banks over this interval. For a description of the financial effects of Subchapter S status, see Harvey and Padget (2000).

[19] This variable is similar to a core deposit ratio but excludes small time deposits.

investment securities divided by total assets. Higher values of this ratio imply greater liquidity and a lower downgrade risk, so the expected coefficient sign of this variable is negative.

The next two variables in table 1 are crude indicators of interest rate risk. Both have total assets in the denominator. The first ratio has total loans that mature or reprice in five or more years in the numerator. The second ratio substitutes total assets that mature or reprice in five years or more in the numerator. Higher values of these ratios imply more interest rate risk and so the expected coefficients of each are positive.

The ratio of net gains on loans sold divided by total assets was found to be significant with a positive sign in Whalen (2005) when the 1997 model was estimated. This variable had not been found to be an important determinant of bank risk in other early warning studies. One possible explanation for a positive coefficient is that supervisors view loan sales as a nearly last resort of banks with weakening performance. It could also reflect a belief that the quality of the retained loan portfolio is being reduced by the sale of higher quality assets.

A measure of bank size, the log of total assets appears in the 1997 and 1999 models with a negative significant coefficient implying that larger size is associated with lower downgrade risk. This result probably reflects an actual or perceived size-related diversification benefit.

The final variable that appears in four of the five models is an indicator of management quality, derived from proprietary exam data. This variable is a dummy variable and takes on a value of one for banks where the management component score exceeds its overall CAMELS composite rating. Because higher values indicate greater risk in this rating system, banks with values of 1 for this variable have relatively lower management quality. Banks with lower management quality are more likely to suffer downgrades in their composite rating, so the coefficient on this variable is expected to be positive.

V. Analysis of Model Accuracy

The most meaningful test of the classification accuracy of any EWM is how well it identifies high- and low-risk banks out-of-sample.[20] To evaluate classification accuracy, predicted risk classifications must be generated using the estimated models and compared with actual classifications. Technically the estimated survivor functions can produce estimates of the likelihood that a bank with a given set of characteristics will survive any number of quarters up to a maximum of eight without being downgraded. This paper focuses on the last quarter of the interval or alternatively on predictions of the probability that a bank with some set of characteristics is not downgraded over the ensuing eight quarters.

To obtain predicted risk classifications, a critical survival probability cutoff threshold must be selected to separate banks with predicted high downgrade risk from those with low risk. Banks with predicted survival probabilities less than or equal to the critical cutoff value are classified as high risk or predicted downgrades. Those with predicted survival probabilities above the critical value are classified as low risk or predicted not to be non-downgraded. Once this classification process is completed, these predictions can be compared with actual outcomes to determine the frequency of correct and incorrect classifications made using each model.

There are two types of classification error that can be made using an EWM. One, labeled a Type I error, occurs when the model predictions fail to correctly identify true high-risk banks. In this study, this means classifying an actual downgrade as a non-downgrade. A Type II error results when the model misclassifies a true low-risk bank as high risk. Here this means predicting a downgrade for a bank that does not actually occur. Both of these sorts of errors are of concern when analyzing the accuracy of EWMs. The costs of Type I errors are obvious. But if off-site

---

[20] That is using the estimated model to predict downgrades for banks held out of the estimation sample or data from sample banks over a different time period.

EWMs are used to assist in the allocation of supervisory resources, they should not incorrectly flag large numbers of true low-risk banks as warranting closer scrutiny. As a result, the most desirable EWMs have low Type I and Type II error rates.[21]

Analysis of the accuracy of EWMs is complicated because changing the probability cutoff value used to make the predicted risk classifications changes the number of predicted high-risk and low-risk banks. Raising the critical survival probability cutoff value implies more predicted downgrades, and vice versa. As a result, the measured classification accuracy of this or any other EWM varies with the chosen probability cutoff.

One way to proceed is to examine forecast accuracy using some judgmentally chosen probability cutoff value or range of values.[22] An alternative is to calculate all possible combinations of Type I and Type II error rates produced by the model as the classification cutoff value is allowed to vary over virtually all of its entire range from 0 to 1. The graph of all of these pairs of error rates is known as a power curve. This is the basic approach taken here and is described in more detail below.

The forecasting exercise in this paper is designed to closely resemble the process that would be used if this sort of EWM were actually employed by supervisors. For example, the 1997 model could be estimated only after downgrade information through the end of the first quarter of 2000 was available. Thus this model would be available for forecasting only after that date. It seems reasonable to assume that it could be used when 2000 final year-end call-report

---

[21] Accuracy is analyzed in terms of error rates rather than number of errors because the number of high- and low-risk banks in a given sample may differ considerably. The Type I error rate is the number of true high-risk banks missed by the model divided by the total number of true high-risk banks in the sample. The Type II error rate is defined similarly.

[22] For example, often the probability is set equal to the relative frequency of high-risk or low-risk banks observed in the estimation sample.

data for the explanatory variables were available.[23] Similarly, estimation of the 1999 model requires 2002:Q1 downgrade information and so should be available for use by the end of 2002. To reflect the realistic data requirements for each model, the probability that a sample bank would not be downgraded by the end of the eight-quarter time period is computed for year-end dates where that model would have been available. The first year-end forecast date examined is 2002, and the last is 2007.[24] For each model in each forecast year, the sample banks are ranked from predicted lowest survival probability (highest downgrade risk) to highest survival probability (lowest downgrade risk) at an eight-quarter time horizon. Next, the probability cutoff value is alternatively assumed to be equal to each predicted ascending survival probability value observed. For each successive threshold, all banks with probabilities of not being downgraded equal to or less than that threshold are predicted to be high risk, and those with probabilities above this value are predicted to be low risk. The implied Type I and Type II error rates produced by the model for each cutoff value are then computed.

This exercise amounts to creating a series of ever larger supervisory "watch lists" where each list includes all banks with probabilities less than or equal to each respective survival probability threshold value. The risk-ranking data also reveal how many true high-risk and low-risk banks will be on a watch list of any given size. More accurate models will correctly identify a given percentage of true high-risk banks with a shorter watch list. Alternatively, more accurate models have a lower Type II error rate for any given Type I error rate.

---

[23] Typically, final call-report data are available roughly 45 days after the end of each calendar quarter.

[24] 2007 is the last year-end forecast period examined because actual downgrade data beyond 2010:Q1 were not yet available when this analysis was done.

Accuracy of Hazard Downgrade Models

Tables 2 through 6 provide information on the out-of-sample classification accuracy of the five models. A separate panel in each table contains the risk classification results obtained using a given model to predict bank risk for each feasible forecast year. The total number of actual downgrades, non-downgrades, ultimate failures, and downgraded ultimate failures in the sample for each forecast period appear at the top of each panel. The second and fourth columns in each panel show the Type I and Type II error rates associated with five watch lists of relatively small size based on the ranked estimated downgrade probabilities of the model in a given year. Thus, the pairs of error rates in each panel represent five of the points on the model's complete power curve for that forecast year. The watch-list sizes used in the tables were chosen because they imply heightened scrutiny of roughly 20 percent to 33 percent of low-risk community national banks in a given year, which represents a practicable and reasonably cheap supervisory strategy.

In addition to the conventional error rates, the last three columns of each table contain supplemental information that provides additional insight into the forecasting accuracy of the models, given that they are based on supervisory assessments of bank risk. The fifth column in each table shows the number of community national banks in the forecast sample on each watch list that ultimately failed after the start of the forecast period through June 1, 2010.[25] Column six shows the number of ultimate failures on each watch list that were actually downgraded during the forecast period. The differences between the numbers in columns five and six for each watch-list size reveal the number of Type II errors in the forecast year that turned out to be very high-

---

[25] This is the date when this analysis was completed. Most of the sample banks categorized as ultimate failures in this study were closed after 2008. For example, of the 25 ultimate failures in the 2002 data set, 15 failed in 2009 and 5 more failed in early 2010.

risk banks in the more distant future. This sort of error suggests that the associated conventional Type II error rates reported in some panels are overstated to some extent.

The last column of each panel shows the number of banks on each watch list considered to be Type II errors in the forecast period that were actually downgraded during the next four quarters after the end of the forecast period.[26] The short time interval between the end of the forecast period and these near-term subsequent downgrades suggests that model classification of these banks as higher risk in the forecast period was not wrong and so the true Type II error rate is lower than the percentage reported in the table.

In general, the results in tables 2 through 6 suggest a watch list size of 500 banks is necessary to produce Type I error rates below 40 percent. As a result, the key classification accuracy measures for each model in each feasible forecast year for this watch-list size are reported together in the six panels of table 7. Each panel of table 7 includes the Type I error rate, the Type II error rate, the number of ultimate failures flagged as high risk, and the number of Type II errors downgraded in the four quarters after the end of the forecast period for the relevant set of models for a particular forecast year. The associated accuracy rank for each measure (with 1 indicating highest accuracy) is also reported. Combining the classification statistics for all of the models in a single table makes it easier to compare the accuracy of the alternative models over time.

---

[26] For example, when risk forecasts are produced using year-end 2000 data, the set of near-term subsequent downgrades includes banks downgraded from 2005:Q2 through 2006:Q1.

Table 2

1997 Model Accuracy Measures

Forecast Rankings Produced Using 2002:Q4 Data, for Downgrades From 2003:Q2 to 2005:Q1

Sample totals: No. of downgrades: 71   No. of non-downgrades: 1,549   No. of ultimate failures: 25   No. of ultimate failures with downgrades: 1

Watch list size	No. of downgrades on list	Type I error rate	No. of non-downgrades on list	Type II error rate	No. of ultimate failures on list	No. of ultimate failures on list with downgrade	No. of Type II errors on list downgraded in next 4 post-forecast quarters
300	41	0.4225	259	0.1672	12	1	9
350	46	0.3521	304	0.1963	12	1	9
400	48	0.3239	352	0.2272	13	1	10
450	49	0.3099	401	0.2589	16	1	11
500	50	0.2958	450	0.2905	16	1	12

Forecast Rankings Produced Using 2003:Q4 Data, for Downgrades From 2004:Q2 to 2006:Q1

Sample totals: No. of downgrades: 75   No. of non-downgrades: 1,488   No. of ultimate failures: 25   No. of ultimate failures with downgrades: 1

Watch list size	No. of downgrades on list	Type I error rate	No. of non-downgrades on list	Type II error rate	No. of ultimate failures on list	No. of ultimate failures on list with downgrade	No. of Type II errors on list downgraded in next 4 post-forecast quarters
300	28	0.6267	272	0.1828	10	1	6
350	32	0.5733	318	0.2137	11	1	6
400	37	0.5067	363	0.2440	13	1	6
450	41	0.4533	409	0.2749	13	1	7
500	46	0.3867	454	0.3051	15	1	9

Forecast Rankings Produced Using 2004:Q4 Data, for Downgrades From 2005:Q2 to 2007:Q1

Sample totals: No. of downgrades: 66   No. of non-downgrades: 1,467   No. of ultimate failures: 26   No. of ultimate failures with downgrades: 2

Watch list size	No. of downgrades on list	Type I error rate	No. of non-downgrades on list	Type II error rate	No. of ultimate failures on list	No. of ultimate failures on list with downgrade	No. of Type II errors on list downgraded in next 4 post-forecast quarters
300	29	0.5606	271	0.1847	11	1	10
350	32	0.5152	318	0.2168	11	1	12
400	34	0.4848	366	0.2495	13	1	13
450	36	0.4545	414	0.2822	16	1	16
500	38	0.4242	462	0.3149	16	1	17

Table 2 (continued)

1997 Model Accuracy Measures

Forecast Rankings Produced Using 2005:Q4 Data, for Downgrades From 2006:Q2 to 2008:Q1

Sample Totals: No. of downgrades: 50   No. of non-downgrades: 1,389   No. of ultimate failures: 24   No. of ultimate failures with downgrades: 3

Watch list size	No. of downgrades on list	Type I error rate	No. of non-downgrades on list	Type II error rate	No. of ultimate failures on list	No. of ultimate failures on list with downgrade	No. of Type II errors on list downgraded in next 4 post-forecast quarters
300	26	0.4800	274	0.1973	8	2	40
350	26	0.4800	324	0.2333	8	2	46
400	27	0.4600	373	0.2685	12	2	53
450	30	0.4000	420	0.3024	12	2	58
500	33	0.3400	467	0.3362	14	2	63

Forecast Rankings Produced Using 2006:Q4 Data, for Downgrades From 2007:Q2 to 2009:Q1

Sample totals: No. of downgrades: 152   No. of non-downgrades: 1,216   No. of ultimate failures: 22   No. of ultimate failures with downgrades: 18

Watch list size	No. of downgrades on list	Type I error rate	No. of non-downgrades on list	Type II error rate	No. of ultimate failures on list	No. of ultimate failures on list with downgrade	No. of Type II errors on list downgraded in next 4 post-forecast quarters
300	74	0.5132	226	0.1859	9	9	48
350	78	0.4868	272	0.2237	9	9	57
400	84	0.4474	316	0.2599	11	11	62
450	89	0.4145	361	0.2969	11	11	70
500	97	0.3618	403	0.3314	11	11	73

Forecast Rankings Produced Using 2007:Q4 Data, for Downgrades From 2008:Q2 to 2010:Q1

Sample totals: No. of downgrades: 282   No. of non-downgrades: 1,001   No. of ultimate failures: 20   No. of ultimate failures with downgrades: 19

Watch list size	No. of downgrades on list	Type I error rate	No. of non-downgrades on list	Type II error rate	No. of ultimate failures on list	No. of ultimate failures on list with downgrade	No. of Type II errors on list downgraded in next 4 post-forecast quarters
300	141	0.5000	159	0.1588	14	14	N/A*
350	155	0.4504	195	0.1948	16	16	N/A
400	165	0.4149	235	0.2348	17	17	N/A
450	173	0.3865	277	0.2767	17	17	N/A
500	182	0.3546	318	0.3177	18	18	N/A

*N/A means not available.

Table 3

1999 Model Accuracy Measures

Forecast Rankings Produced Using 2002:Q4 Data, for Downgrades From 2003:Q2 to 2005:Q1

Sample totals: No. of downgrades: 71   No. of non-downgrades: 1,549   No. of ultimate failures: 25   No. of ultimate failures with downgrade: 1

Watch list size	No. of downgrades on list	Type I error rate	No. of non-downgrades on list	Type II error rate	No. of ultimate failures on list	No. of ultimate failures on list with downgrade	No. of Type II errors on list downgraded in next 4 post-forecast quarters
300	37	0.4789	263	0.1698	10	1	10
350	40	0.4366	310	0.2001	11	1	11
400	43	0.3944	357	0.2305	13	1	12
450	47	0.3380	403	0.2602	15	1	14
500	49	0.3099	451	0.2912	15	1	15

Forecast Rankings Produced Using 2003:Q4 Data, for Downgrades From 2004:Q2 to 2006:Q1

Sample totals: No. of downgrades: 75   No. of non-downgrades: 1,488   No. of ultimate failures: 25   No. of ultimate failures with downgrade: 1

Watch list size	No. of downgrades on list	Type I error rate	No. of non-downgrades on list	Type II error rate	No. of ultimate failures on list	No. of ultimate failures on list with downgrade	No. of Type II errors on list downgraded in next 4 post-forecast quarters
300	29	0.6133	271	0.1821	10	1	7
350	35	0.5333	315	0.2117	11	1	7
400	39	0.4800	361	0.2426	11	1	9
450	44	0.4133	406	0.2728	11	1	9
500	45	0.4000	455	0.3058	12	1	9

Forecast Rankings Produced Using 2004:Q4 Data, for Downgrades From 2005:Q2 to 2007:Q1

Sample totals: No. of downgrades: 66   No. of non-downgrades: 1,467   No. of ultimate failures: 26   No. of ultimate failures with downgrade: 2

Watch list size	No. of downgrades on list	Type I error rate	No. of non-downgrades on list	Type II error rate	No. of ultimate failures on list	No. of ultimate failures on list with downgrade	No. of Type II errors on list downgraded in next 4 post-forecast quarters
300	31	0.5303	269	0.1834	10	1	9
350	34	0.4848	316	0.2154	12	1	11
400	39	0.4091	361	0.2461	13	1	13
450	40	0.3939	410	0.2795	13	1	17
500	45	0.3182	455	0.3102	14	1	17

Table 3 (continued)

1999 Model Accuracy Measures

Forecast Rankings Produced Using 2005:Q4 Data, for Downgrades From 2006:Q2 to 2008:Q1

Sample totals: No. of downgrades: 50   No. of non-downgrades: 1,389   No. of ultimate failures: 25   No. of ultimate failures with downgrade: 3

Watch list size	No. of downgrades on list	Type I error rate	No. of non-downgrades on list	Type II error rate	No. of ultimate failures on list	No. of ultimate failures on list with downgrade	No. of Type II errors on list downgraded in next 4 post-forecast quarters
300	25	0.5000	275	0.1980	11	2	39
350	27	0.4600	323	0.2325	12	2	47
400	29	0.4200	371	0.2671	13	2	52
450	32	0.3600	418	0.3009	15	2	57
500	35	0.3000	465	0.3348	16	2	64

Forecast Rankings Produced Using 2006:Q4 Data, for Downgrades From 2007:Q2 to 2009:Q1

Sample totals: No. of downgrades: 152   No. of non-downgrades: 1,216   No. of ultimate failures: 22   No. of ultimate failures with downgrade: 18

Watch list size	No. of downgrades on list	Type I error rate	No. of non-downgrades on list	Type II error rate	No. of ultimate failures on list	No. of ultimate failures on list with downgrade	No. of Type II errors on list downgraded in next 4 post-forecast quarters
300	67	0.5592	233	0.1916	8	7	52
350	72	0.5263	278	0.2286	9	8	59
400	83	0.4539	317	0.2607	13	12	62
450	92	0.3947	358	0.2944	14	13	65
500	100	0.3421	400	0.3289	15	14	68

Forecast Rankings Produced Using 2007:Q4 Data, for Downgrades From 2008:Q2 to 2010:Q1

Sample totals: No. of downgrades: 282   No. of non-downgrades: 1,001   No. of ultimate failures: 20   No. of ultimate failures with downgrade: 18

Watch list size	No. of downgrades on list	Type I error rate	No. of non-downgrades on list	Type II error rate	No. of ultimate failures on list	No. of ultimate failures on list with downgrade	No. of Type II errors on list downgraded in next 4 post-forecast quarters
300	136	0.5177	164	0.1638	13	13	N/A*
350	151	0.4645	199	0.1988	13	13	N/A
400	160	0.4326	240	0.2398	13	13	N/A
450	170	0.3972	280	0.2797	15	15	N/A
500	183	0.3511	317	0.3167	15	15	N/A

*N/A means not available.

Table 4

2000 Model Accuracy Measures

Forecast Rankings Produced Using 2003:Q4 Data, for Downgrades From 2004:Q2 to 2006:Q1

Sample totals: No. of downgrades: 75 No. of non-downgrades: 1488 No. of ultimate failures: 25 No. of ultimate failures with downgrade: 1

Watch list size	No. of downgrades on list	Type I error rate	No. of non-downgrades on list	Type II error rate	No. of ultimate failures on list	No. of ultimate failures on list with downgrade	No. of Type II errors on list downgraded in next 4 post-forecast quarters
300	35	0.5333	265	0.1781	11	1	4
350	38	0.4933	312	0.2097	13	1	6
400	41	0.4533	359	0.2413	14	1	7
450	42	0.4400	408	0.2742	16	1	9
500	45	0.4000	455	0.3058	18	1	9

Forecast Rankings Produced Using 2004:Q4 Data, for Downgrades From 2005:Q2 to 2007:Q1

Sample totals: No. of downgrades: 66 No. of non-downgrades: 1467 No. of ultimate failures: 26 No. of ultimate failures with downgrade: 2

Watch list size	No. of downgrades on list	Type I error rate	No. of non-downgrades on list	Type II error rate	No. of ultimate failures on list	No. of ultimate failures on list with downgrade	No. of Type II errors on list downgraded in next 4 post-forecast quarters
300	31	0.5303	269	0.1834	13	1	10
350	36	0.4545	314	0.2140	13	1	12
400	38	0.4242	362	0.2468	17	1	13
450	43	0.3485	407	0.2774	17	1	14
500	44	0.3333	456	0.3108	18	1	15

Forecast Rankings Produced Using 2005:Q4 Data, for Downgrades From 2006:Q2 to 2008:Q1

Sample totals: No. of downgrades: 50 No. of non-downgrades: 1389 No. of ultimate failures: 24 No. of ultimate failures with downgrade: 3

Watch list size	No. of downgrades on list	Type I error rate	No. of non-downgrades on list	Type II error rate	No. of ultimate failures on list	No. of ultimate failures on list with downgrade	No. of Type II errors on list downgraded in next 4 post-forecast quarters
300	23	0.5400	277	0.1994	14	2	53
350	29	0.4200	321	0.2311	14	2	58
400	34	0.3200	366	0.2635	16	2	64
450	35	0.3000	415	0.2988	17	2	67
500	37	0.2600	463	0.3333	17	2	73

Table 4 (continued)

2000 Model Accuracy Measures

Forecast Rankings Produced Using 2006:Q4 Data, for Downgrades From 2007:Q2 to 2009:Q1

Sample totals: No. of downgrades: 152   No. of non-downgrades: 1216   No. of ultimate failures: 22   No. of ultimate failures with downgrade: 18

Watch list size	No. of downgrades on list	Type I error rate	No. of non-downgrades on list	Type II error rate	No. of ultimate failures on list	No. of ultimate failures on list with downgrade	No. of Type II errors on list downgraded in next 4 post-forecast quarters
300	76	0.5000	224	0.1842	11	10	47
350	78	0.4868	272	0.2237	12	10	56
400	83	0.4539	317	0.2607	13	11	68
450	90	0.4079	360	0.2961	13	11	78
500	95	0.3750	405	0.3331	15	13	84

Forecast Rankings Produced Using 2007:Q4 Data, for Downgrades From 2008:Q2 to 2010:Q1

Sample totals: No. of downgrades: 282   No. of non-downgrades: 1001   No. of ultimate failures: 20   No. of ultimate failures with downgrade: 19

Watch list size	No. of downgrades on list	Type I error rate	No. of non-downgrades on list	Type II error rate	No. of ultimate failures on list	No. of ultimate failures on list with downgrade	No. of Type II errors on list downgraded in next 4 post-forecast quarters
300	141	0.5000	159	0.1588	11	11	N/A*
350	157	0.4433	193	0.1928	11	11	N/A
400	170	0.3972	230	0.2298	13	13	N/A
450	184	0.3475	266	0.2657	14	14	N/A
500	194	0.3121	306	0.3057	15	15	N/A

*N/A means not available.

Table 5

2001 Model Accuracy Measures

Forecast Rankings Produced Using 2004:Q4 Data, for Downgrades From 2005:Q2 to 2007:Q1

Sample totals: No. of downgrades: 66 No. of non-downgrades: 1467 No. of ultimate failures: 26 No. of ultimate failures with downgrade: 2

Watch list size	No. of downgrades on list	Type I error rate	No. of non-downgrades on list	Type II error rate	No. of ultimate failures on list	No. of ultimate failures on list with downgrade	No. of Type II errors on list downgraded in next 4 post-forecast quarters
300	35	0.4697	265	0.1806	10	1	8
350	36	0.4545	314	0.2140	11	1	9
400	36	0.4545	364	0.2481	13	1	13
450	37	0.4394	413	0.2815	14	1	15
500	40	0.3939	460	0.3136	15	1	16

Forecast Rankings Produced Using 2005:Q4 Data, for Downgrades From 2006:Q2 to 2008:Q1

Sample totals: No. of downgrades: 50 No. of non-downgrades: 1389 No. of ultimate failures: 24 No. of ultimate failures with downgrade: 3

Watch list size	No. of downgrades on list	Type I error rate	No. of non-downgrades on list	Type II error rate	No. of ultimate failures on list	No. of ultimate failures on list with downgrade	No. of Type II errors on list downgraded in next 4 post-forecast quarters
300	23	0.5400	277	0.1994	9	2	41
350	24	0.5200	326	0.2347	12	2	46
400	27	0.4600	373	0.2685	13	2	47
450	31	0.3800	419	0.3017	14	2	54
500	37	0.2600	463	0.3333	15	2	57

Forecast Rankings Produced Using 2006:Q4 Data, for Downgrades From 2007:Q2 to 2009:Q1

Sample totals: No. of downgrades: 152 No. of non-downgrades: 1216 No. of ultimate failures: 22 No. of ultimate failures with downgrade: 18

Watch list size	No. of downgrades on list	Type I error rate	No. of non-downgrades on list	Type II error rate	No. of ultimate failures on list	No. of ultimate failures on list with downgrade	No. of Type II errors on list downgraded in next 4 post-forecast quarters
300	66	0.5658	234	0.1924	10	10	44
350	74	0.5132	276	0.2270	11	11	51
400	87	0.4276	313	0.2574	11	11	55
450	92	0.3947	358	0.2944	11	11	61
500	99	0.3487	401	0.3298	13	13	69

Forecast Rankings Produced Using 2007:Q4 Data, for Downgrades From 2008:Q2 to 2010:Q1

Sample totals: No. of downgrades: 282 No. of non-downgrades: 1001 No. of ultimate failures: 20 No. of ultimate failures with downgrade: 18

Watch list size	No. of downgrades on list	Type I error rate	No. of non-downgrades on list	Type II error rate	No. of ultimate failures on list	No. of ultimate failures on list with downgrade	No. of Type II errors on list downgraded in next 4 post-forecast quarters
300	134	0.5248	166	0.1658	12	12	N/A*
350	150	0.4681	200	0.1998	12	12	N/A
400	167	0.4078	233	0.2328	14	14	N/A
450	178	0.3688	272	0.2717	15	15	N/A
500	191	0.3227	309	0.3087	15	15	N/A

*N/A means not available.

Table 6

2002 Model Accuracy Measures

Forecast Rankings Produced Using 2005:Q4 Data, for Downgrades From 2006:Q2 to 2008:Q1

Sample totals: No. of downgrades: 50   No. of non-downgrades: 1389   No. of ultimate failures: 24   No. of ultimate failures with downgrade: 3

Watch list size	No. of downgrades on list	Type I error rate	No. of non-downgrades on list	Type II error rate	No. of ultimate failures on list	No. of ultimate failures on list with downgrade	No. of Type II errors on list downgraded in next 4 post-forecast quarters
300	25	0.5000	275	0.1980	8	2	41
350	31	0.3800	319	0.2297	9	2	45
400	31	0.3800	369	0.2657	14	2	53
450	31	0.3800	419	0.3017	16	2	59
500	32	0.3600	468	0.3369	18	2	66

Forecast Rankings Produced Using 2006:Q4 Data, for Downgrades From 2007:Q2 to 2009:Q1

Sample totals: No. of downgrades: 152   No. of non-downgrades: 1216   No. of ultimate failures: 22   No. of ultimate failures with downgrade: 18

Watch list size	No. of downgrades on list	Type I error rate	No. of non-downgrades on list	Type II error rate	No. of ultimate failures on list	No. of ultimate failures on list with downgrade	No. of Type II errors on list downgraded in next 4 post-forecast quarters
300	70	0.5395	230	0.1891	10	10	42
350	79	0.4803	271	0.2229	11	11	52
400	84	0.4474	316	0.2599	11	11	59
450	93	0.3882	357	0.2936	14	14	65
500	95	0.3750	405	0.3331	14	14	72

Forecast Rankings Produced Using 2007:Q4 Data, for Downgrades From 2008:Q2 to 2010:Q1

Sample totals: No. of downgrades: 282   No. of non-downgrades: 1001   No. of ultimate failures: 20   No. of ultimate failures with downgrade: 19

Watch list size	No. of downgrades on list	Type I error rate	No. of non-downgrades on list	Type II error rate	No. of ultimate failures on list	No. of ultimate failures on list with downgrade	No. of Type II errors on list downgraded in next 4 post-forecast quarters
300	141	0.5000	159	0.1588	16	16	N/A*
350	158	0.4397	192	0.1918	16	16	N/A
400	173	0.3865	227	0.2268	17	17	N/A
450	185	0.3440	265	0.2647	17	17	N/A
500	195	0.3085	305	0.3047	17	17	N/A

*N/A means not available.

The forecasting accuracy of the 1997 model for six different forecast periods is documented in the first two columns of the six panels of table 7. It is not surprising that the minimum Type I error rate for this model of 29.58 percent is evident in the first forecast year (2002), which is closest to the time period in which the model was estimated. Deterioration in classification accuracy as the time between the estimation and forecasting periods lengthens is expected, and this pattern is evident in 2003 and 2004, where the Type I error rate of the 1997 model increases steadily, hitting 42.42 percent in 2004. What is unexpected is that the upward trend in the Type I error rate stops after 2004. The Type I error rate of the 1997 model is 34 percent in 2005, markedly lower than it is in either 2003 or 2004. The Type I error rates in the two most recent forecast years are just slightly higher than the 2005 value, with a slight decline evident in 2007 relative to 2006. The associated accuracy rankings also show that the Type I error rates of the 1997 model compare quite favorably to the more recently estimated versions. The 1997 model has the highest Type I error rate in only two of the six forecast periods examined.

Table 7

Summary of Model Accuracy Based on 500 Bank Watch List

Forecast Rankings Produced Using 2002:Q4 Data, for Downgrades From 2003:Q2 to 2005:Q1

Sample totals: No. of downgrades: 71   No. of non-downgrades: 1,549   No. of ultimate failures: 25   No. of ultimate failures with downgrade: 1

Accuracy measure	1997 model		1999 model		2000 model		2001 model		2002 model	
	Value	Accuracy rank	Value	Accuracy rank	Value	Accuracy rank	Value	Accuracy rank	Value	Accuracy rank
□□te □ero□ate	0.2958	1	0.3099	2	N/A*	N/A	N/A	N/A	N/A	N/A
□te □ero□ate	0.2905	1	0.2912	2	N/A	N/A	N/A	N/A	N/A	N/A
Number of ultimate failures on list	16	1	15	2	N/A	N/A	N/A	N/A	N/A	N/A
Number of □ero□s on list in net 4 □arte□s	12	2	15	1	N/A	N/A	N/A	N/A	N/A	N/A

Forecast Rankings Produced Using 2003:Q4 Data, for Downgrades From 2004:Q2 to 2006:Q1

Sample totals: No. of downgrades: 75   No. of non-downgrades: 1,488   No. of ultimate failures: 25   No. of ultimate failures with downgrade: 1

Accuracy measure	1997 model		1999 model		2000 model		2001 model		2002 model	
	Value	Accuracy rank	Value	Accuracy rank	Value	Accuracy rank	Value	Accuracy rank	Value	Accuracy rank
□□te □ero□ate	0.3867	1	0.4	2□□□	0.4	2□□□	N/A	N/A	N/A	N/A
□te □ero□ate	0.3051	1	0.3058	2□□□	0.3058	2□□□	N/A	N/A	N/A	N/A
Number of ultimate failures on list	15	2	12	3	18	1	N/A	N/A	N/A	N/A
Number of □ero□s on list in net 4 □arte□s	9	1□□**□	9	1□□□	9	1□□□	N/A	N/A	N/A	N/A

Forecast Rankings Produced Using 2004:Q4 Data, for Downgrades From 2005:Q2 to 2007:Q1

Sample totals: No. of downgrades: 66   No. of non-downgrades: 1,467   No. of ultimate failures: 26   No. of ultimate failures with downgrade: 2

Accuracy measure	1997 model		1999 model		2000 model		2001 model		2002 model	
	Value	Accuracy rank	Value	Accuracy rank	Value	Accuracy rank	Value	Accuracy rank	Value	Accuracy rank
□□te □ero□ate	0.4242	4	0.3182	1	0.3333	2	0.3939	3	N/A	N/A
□te □ero□ate	0.3149	4	0.3102	1	0.3108	2	0.3136	3	N/A	N/A
Number of ultimate failures on list	16	2	14	4	18	1	15	3	N/A	N/A
Number of □ero□s on list in net 4 □arte□s	17	1□□□	17	1□□□	15	3	16	2	N/A	N/A

*N/A means not available.

**□ means t□e □an□in□s a□e tie□.

30

Table 7 (continued)

Summary of Model Accuracy Based on 500 Bank Watchlist

Forecast Rankings Produced Using 2005:Q4 Data, For Downgrades From 2006:Q2 to 2008:Q1

Sample totals: No. of downgrades: 50   No. of non-downgrades: 1,389   No. of ultimate failures: 24   No. of ultimate failures with downgrade: 3

Accuracy measure	1997 model		1999 model		2000 model		2001 model		2002 model	
	Value	Accuracy rank	Value	Accuracy rank	Value	Accuracy rank	Value	Accuracy rank	Value	Accuracy rank
Type I error rate	0.3400	3	0.3000	2	0.2600	1**	0.2600	1**	0.3600	4
Type II error rate	0.3362	3	0.3348	2	0.3333	1**	0.3333	1**	0.3369	4
Number of ultimate failures on list	14	5	16	3	17	2	15	4	18	1
Number of models contained in next 4 quarters	63	4	64	3	73	1	57	5	66	2

Forecast Rankings Produced Using 2006:Q4 Data, for Downgrades From 2007:Q2 to 2009:Q1

Sample totals: No. of downgrades: 152   No. of non-downgrades: 1,216   No. of ultimate failures: 22   No. of ultimate failures with downgrade: 18

Accuracy measure	1997 model		1999 model		2000 model		2001 model		2002 model	
	Value	Accuracy rank	Value	Accuracy rank	Value	Accuracy rank	Value	Accuracy rank	Value	Accuracy rank
Type I error rate	0.3618	3	0.3421	1	0.375	4**	0.3487	2	0.375	4**
Type II error rate	0.3314	3	0.3289	1	0.3331	4	0.3298	2	0.3333	5
Number of ultimate failures on list	11	4	15	1**	15	1**	12	3	14	2
Number of models contained in next 4 quarters	73	2	68	5	84	1	69	4	72	3

Forecast Rankings Produced Using 2007:Q4 Data, for Downgrades From 2008:Q2 to 2010:Q1

Sample totals: No. of downgrades: 282   No. of non-downgrades: 1,001   No. of ultimate failures: 20   No. of ultimate failures with downgrade: 19

Accuracy measure	1997 model		1999 model		2000 model		2001 model		2002 model	
	Value	Accuracy rank	Value	Accuracy rank	Value	Accuracy rank	Value	Accuracy rank	Value	Accuracy rank
Type I error rate	0.3546	5	0.3511	4	0.3121	2	0.3227	3	0.3085	1
Type II error rate	0.3177	5	0.3167	4	0.3057	2	0.3087	3	0.3047	1
Number of ultimate failures on list	18	1	15	3**	15	3**	15	3**	17	2
Number of models contained in next 4 quarters	N/A*	N/A	N/A	N/A	N/A	N/A	N/A	N/A	N/A	N/A

*N/A means not available.
** means the rankings are tied.

31

The Type II error rates of the 1997 model do not change much over the forecast years, hovering in the low 30 percent range. The supplemental information in the next two rows of each panel of table 7 suggests that the true Type II error rate of the 1997 model is less than the reported figure in a number of forecast periods. For example, the number in the third row of the first panel of table 7 indicates that 16 of the 25 (64 percent) sample banks that ultimately failed by June 1, 2010, appear on the 500-bank watch list produced using year-end 2002 data in the 1997 model. Corresponding data in column 6 in the first panel of table 2 show that only 1 of these banks was actually downgraded during the forecast period. Thus 15 of the 16 ultimate failures identified by the 1997 model are categorized as Type II errors for the 2002 forecast period. These 15 banks represent 3.3 percent of the total number of such errors (15/450) in this time period.

The data in the last row of column 7 provide additional evidence that the true Type II error rates for the 1997 model may be lower than the stated values. The reported value of 12 represents the number of banks categorized as Type II errors for the forecast period that were actually downgraded during the four quarters that immediately followed.[27] The relatively short time period between the end of the forecast period and their subsequent downgrade suggests that their relatively high-risk ranking by the model was correct. These 12 banks represent 2.7 percent (12/450) of the reported number of Type II errors produced by the 1997 model for the 2002 forecasting period.

There is virtually no overlap between these two groups of possibly misclassified Type II errors for the 1997 model forecast for 2002.[28] That means that the reported Type II error rate is roughly five percentage points above the true rate.

---

[27] For example, in the first panel of table 2, 2002 year-end data for the explanatory variables are used to forecast downgrades over the eight-quarter period from 2003:Q2 through 2005:Q1. The data in column 7 are the number of banks on the 2002 watch list that were downgraded over the period from 2005:Q2 through 2006:Q1.
[28] Only one Type II error bank that ultimately failed is also included in the downgrade count over the next four quarters.

The number of ultimate failures and near-term post-forecast period downgrades included on the watch lists for the next three forecast years all show that a considerable number of the 1997 model's apparent Type II errors do turn out to be relatively risky in post-forecast periods. For example, the numbers of ultimately failing banks classified as Type II errors by the 1997 model are 14, 15 and 12 in 2003, 2004, and 2005, respectively. The Type II error counts in these three years also include 9, 17 and 63 banks downgraded in the first four post-forecast quarters. Again there is limited overlap in these two groups of sample banks in all three forecast years, implying that the model is a bit more accurate than indicated by the conventional Type II error rates.[29]

The accuracy rankings related to the counts of early identification of ultimate failures and downgrades indicate that the 1997 model performs relatively well compared with newer competing models over time. The 1997 model has the lowest accuracy in only one case (the number of ultimate failures on the watch list in the 2005 forecast period), and the deficiency in this instance is relatively small.[30] In 2007, the 1997 model identifies the second-highest number of near-term subsequent downgrades and in 2008 the largest number of ultimate failures.

The next two columns of table 7 contain the risk classification results for the 1999 model for the same six forecast years. The data in table 7 generally reveal modest differences in Type I and Type II error rates when the 1999 model and 1997 model are compared in each period. The lone exception is 2004 when the 1999 model Type I error rate is about 10 percentage points lower. In the first two forecast years, the older 1997 model has a slightly lower Type I error rate.

---

[29] The number of banks common to the ultimate failure and near-term subsequent downgrade groups is 0 in 2003, 2 in 2004, and 10 in 2005.

[30] The 1997 model flags one fewer ultimate failure than the next best model (14 versus 15) and four fewer than the top-ranked model.

The 1999 model does a better job than the 1997 model in correctly identifying actual downgrades in the three most recent forecast periods, but the Type I error rate improvement is never more than 4 percentage points (in 2005), and in 2007 it is just 4 basis points. These results indicate that decreasing the age of this type of EWM by two years (and incurring the associated development expenses) does not yield a large return in the form of increased accuracy. Alternatively, the results do confirm the finding that a fairly old EWM can produce decent forecasts of downgrade risk well beyond its estimation period. The associated accuracy rankings show that the 1999 model compares favorably with newer models in terms of Type I and Type II error rates in several of the most recent forecast periods. For example, the 1999 model has the second-lowest Type I error rate of the five models examined in 2005, and the lowest in 2006.

In table 7, the supplemental classification information in the last two rows of each panel shows that the numbers of ultimate failures and near-term subsequent downgrades erroneously flagged as high risk by the 1999 model in each forecast year are close to the comparable figures for the 1997 model. One interesting difference is that the older model flags slightly more of the ultimate failures as high risk in four of the six forecast years. In general, these data imply that the Type II error rates of the 1999 model are inflated to a similar extent.

The classification results obtained using the 2000 model for the five feasible forecast years are summarized in the next two columns of table 7. The out-of-sample forecasting performance of this model is not clearly and consistently superior to that of the two older models. The 2000 model has a lower Type I error rate than both older models in only two of the five forecast years (2005 and 2007). The accuracy rankings also suggest that this pattern persists when the 2000 model is compared with the two newer models. Of the seven possible comparisons in the Type I error rates of the 2000 model versus the 2001 and 2002 models, the 2000 error rate is higher in only two cases.[31]

The 2000 model generally identifies at least as many ultimate failures and near-term subsequent downgrades as high risk in each forecast year as the two older models and in some years flags more, implying similar levels of possible Type II error overstatement.. The modest improvement in accuracy in identifying these sorts of banks is interesting because the 2000 model specification is the only one of the five estimated that does not include an equity capital measure as an explanatory variable.

The out-of-sample classification accuracy of the 2001 model is summarized in the next two columns of table 7. The Type I error rate of the 2001 model is lower than that of the oldest model in all four comparison years, although the size of the advantage is typically modest. But the 2001 model does not consistently identify higher percentages of actual downgrades than either the 1999 or 2000 vintage models in the forecast periods examined. The Type I error rate of the 2001 model is less than the 1999 model in two of the four forecast periods and below that of the 2000 model in just one.[32]

The numbers of ultimate failures and near-term subsequent downgrades categorized as Type II errors by the 2001 model in each forecast year are not generally higher than the comparable totals flagged by the older models. The model exhibits its best accuracy rank of 2 only once during the four feasible forecast periods.

The final two columns of table 7 contain the forecasting results obtained using the 2002 downgrade model for the years 2005 through 2007. Unlike the older models, this model is

---

[31] The Type I error rate of the 2000 model is higher than the comparable rate of the 2001 model in 2006 and the 2002 model in 2007.

[32] In one year, the Type I error rates of the 2001 and 2000 models are equal.

relatively inaccurate in the forecast periods closest to the time at which it was estimated. Both the Type I and Type II error rates for the 2002 model are higher than the comparable values for the other older models in the first two forecast years, with an accuracy ranking no better than 4 in both periods. The accuracy of this model improves significantly in the most recent forecast year, however, where it has Type I and Type II error rates below those of all other models.

The results in the bottom two rows of the last three panels of table 7 do show that the 2002 model does a fairly good of identifying ultimate failures and near-term subsequent downgrades even in forecast periods when its Type I and Type II error rates are relatively high. For example, the model flags 18 of the 24 (75 percent) ultimate failures in the 2005 forecast period, more than any competing model, when it has the fourth highest Type I error rate. The 2002 model also includes the second-highest number of near-term subsequent downgrades on its watch list in that forecast year.

VI. Summary and Conclusions

This paper examines the out-of-sample forecasting accuracy of a set of Cox proportional hazard composite CAMELS downgrade models estimated at five different year-end dates ranging from 1997 through 2002. The survivor functions of the models are used to predict the probability that a low-risk community bank (composite CAMELS of 1 or 2) will not be downgraded to high-risk status (composite CAMELS of 3, 4, or 5) over an eight-quarter time horizon beginning with the second quarter after the year-end estimation date. The specifications of the models were allowed to differ across the estimation periods, but the set of explanatory variables used in each model was intentionally limited to a small number of statistically significant risk indicators employed in previous empirical work. The intent of this constraint was to investigate the accuracy of simple, low-cost EWMs over time.

36

Beginning in 2002 and ending in 2007, year-end data for the explanatory variables are used in each model to predict the probability of downgrades over the ensuing eight-quarter period for feasible forecast years. Comparing the accuracy of the models over the forecast years yields interesting findings. When the analysis focuses on the 500 riskiest banks identified by the models, the conventional Type I and Type II error rates of all of the models are almost always in the low- to mid-30 percent range in all forecast years, including the most recent one where the models are used to predict downgrades through the first quarter of 2010. Forecast accuracy does not consistently or sharply decline with model age. This pattern indicates that this type of EWM can be a valuable supervisory tool, even if it is not respecified or re-estimated frequently.

In addition, the supplemental analysis of forecast accuracy indicates that a considerable number of banks categorized as Type II errors by the models in each forecast period appear to be high risk ex post. The implication is that the "true" Type II error rates of the models are lower than the conventional figures reported in the tables.

Further research could investigate whether additional data items constructed either from call report or other data sources (e.g., changes in versus levels of the explanatory variables, or indicators of state or local economic conditions) can improve the accuracy of this type of model. Other interesting issues include the impact of augmenting the sample with larger banks or extending the forecast horizon beyond eight quarters.

References

Allison, P. *Survival Analysis Using the SAS System: A Practical Guide.* Cary, NC: SAS Institute, 1995.

Board of Governors of the Federal Reserve System. *Commercial Bank Examination Manual.* Washington, DC: 1997.

Cleves, M., W. Gould, and R. Gutierrez. *An Introduction to Survival Analysis Using Stata.* College Station, Texas: Stata Corporation, 2002.

Feldman, R., and J. Schmidt. "What Are CAMELS and Who Should Know?" *Fedgazette,* Federal Reserve Bank of Minneapolis, January 1999.

Fissel, G. "Risk Measurement, Actuarially-Fair Deposit Insurance Premiums and the FDIC's Risk-Related Premium System." *FDIC Banking Review* 7, no. 1 (1994).

Gropp, R., J. Vesala, and G. Vulpes. "Equity and Bond Market Signals as Leading Indicators of Bank Fragility." Working Paper No. 150, European Central Bank, June 2002.

Harvey, J., and J. Padget. "Subchapter S— – A New Tool for Enhancing the Value of Community Banks." *Financial Industry Perspectives,* Federal Reserve Bank of Kansas City, 2000.

Hosmer, D., and S. Lemeshow. *Applied Survival Analysis.* New York: John Wiley and Sons, 1999.

Lane, W., S. Looney, and J. Wansley. "An Application of the Cox Proportional Hazards Model to Bank Failure." *Journal of Banking and Finance* 10 (December 1986).

Office of the Comptroller of the Currency. "Community Bank Supervision," *Comptroller's Handbook* (January 2010).

Whalen, G. "A Proportional Hazards Model of Bank Failure: An Examination of Its Usefulness as an Early Warning Tool." *Economic Review* 27, no. 1, Federal Reserve Bank of Cleveland, 1991.

——. "A Hazard Model of CAMELS Downgrades of Low-Risk Community Banks." Economics Working Paper 2005-1, Office of the Comptroller of the Currency, May 2005.

Wheelock, D. and P. Wilson. "Why Do Banks Disappear? The Determinants of U.S. Bank Failures and Acquisitions." *Review of Economics and Statistics* 82, no. 1 (February 2000).